Father and Son

DENIZÉ LAUTURE

illustrated by JONATHAN GREEN

PHILOMEL BOOKS • NEW YORK

A NOTE ABOUT THIS BOOK:

Father and Son is set in the low country of South Carolina, the home
of the Gullah people. Some of the scenes I've painted in this book may
not be familiar to readers but are part of Gullah life.

The picture of the father and son carrying wood on their heads
is something you can see three times a day, as men, women, and children
carry pieces of wood and branches in this way to use as fuel in old
wood-burning stoves.

Sweet-potato huts are still used today by people of the low country for
storage and protection of sweet potatoes and yams. The huts are always
cylindrical in shape and made out of pine straw, cornstock, and soil. — J. G.

Each illustration in this book is an oil painting, which was photographed
for transparency, scanned by laser, and then reproduced in full color.

The artist gratefully acknowledges the help of Tim Stamm
in making the transparencies of the artwork for this book.

Text copyright © 1992 by Denizé Lauture
Illustrations copyright © 1992 by Jonathan Green
All rights reserved. This book, or parts thereof, may not be reproduced
in any form without permission in writing from the publisher.
Philomel Books, a division of The Putnam & Grosset Group,
200 Madison Avenue, New York, NY 10016. Published simultaneously in Canada
Printed in Hong Kong by South China Printing Co. (1988) Ltd.
Book design by Gunta Alexander. The text was set in Jenson.

Library of Congress Cataloging-in-Publication Data
Lotu, Denizé. Father and son / Denizé Lauture; illustrated by Jonathan Green.
p.   cm.   Summary: A father and son share special times, walking together along a road.
1. Fathers and sons—Juvenile poetry. 2. Children's poetry, American.
[1. Fathers and sons—Poetry. 2. American poetry.] I. Green, Jonathan, ill.
II. Title.   PR9199.3.L648F38   1992   811'.54—dc20   91-29413 CIP AC
ISBN 0-399-21867-X
10   9   8   7   6   5   4   3   2   1
First Impression

To all children who show great respect and love
to every decent man they meet down the many roads of life.
To all men who understand they must love, adopt,
and give a hand to all children of our poor planet.
And to my children, Charles and Conrad.
—D.L.

I am dedicating this book to my patrons, collectors,
and supporters, and to my family for instilling in me a rich
cultural heritage that serves as the genesis for many
of my paintings.
—J.G.

Father and son
Hand in hand
Up on the road
In the sun,

Their bodies stop
The same breeze,

Bend the same sun rays,

And sway left and right,
And right and left,
At the same time.

They gaze
At the same fruit tree,

Listen
To the same bird song,

And hum
The same melody.

They swing together
The same arm,
Land together
The same foot,

And follow together
The same cloud,
Measuring the same ground.

The shadow of one
Touching
The shadow of the other,

The mind of one
Sparking
The mind of the other,

The heart of one
Reaching out to
The heart of the other,

And the soul of one
Knowing
The soul of the other,

Down the road
In the sun,
Father and son
Hand in hand.